PERCEPTION BUSTER

Change your Perception and Live a New Life

GO TO

WWW NEWUNITYINC.COM

RYLAND G. HILL JR.

DEDICATION

I would like to first thank God for giving me all that I have.

I sincerely want to thank my parents, Ryland G. Hill Sr. and Bertha Mae Hill, for teaching me the value of sacrifice.

I thank my wife, Melernea Joyce, for all her continued love and support.

My grandmother Della has been an immense support to me and taught me the lesson of Service.

I also would like to thank my son, Ryland III, who has been patient with me and all my children and grandchildren.

My brothers, Anthony and Charles's support during my journey helped me greatly as well.

Special thanks to Lisa and Sheldon, and the rest of the team for their editing work on this project.

TABLE OF CONTENTS

ACKNOWLEDGEMENTS

So many wonderful people have supported me through this journey in developing the clarity for "Perception Buster." My sister Carolyn and brother Winstor, who played a pivotal role in my release six years early.

The incredible Dr. Deantoni who listened to me for 3 years and untangled old wounds. She was a great support and encouragement to me. I'm also grateful to Dr. Ray Armstrong, my amazing elementary school Principal who chose me as the nicest and smartest child in the 5th grade.

me in the 5th grade as the smartest and nicest chi

PREFACE

Life is an uphill journey abundant with opportunities. Each has their own experiences to share. And while everyone would have their own story to tell about the path they traveled, we'd notice one thing that would appear common from the stories of the people you would hear. You will learn that rewards and opportunities don't just fall into the laps of people; they are sought.

If you think that life's going to throw at you opportunities while you sit and wait for it, then I hate to break this to you, but you're mistaken. This isn't how it works. This isn't how the world works.

So when we say explore opportunities, what we mean is that you *need* to go out of your way, off the bed, out the door, and walk down a path that you might not have traveled before. Yes, it's *you* who needs to attract opportunities in life. The more you look around, and the more you explore, the more likely you are to hit the right opportunity that might change your life for the better.

How you can look for it, that's what this book is about. This book is for all the Honorable Disabled Discharged Veterans and Returning Citizens with mental health issues, who have worked hard to reinvent their lives while incarcerated. This book is also for all entrepreneurs, aspiring entrepreneurs, leaders, artists, baby boomers, and millennials. It is time to make the necessary steps to create a difference. In these pages, you will "see" why God chose me to write this book. By reading this, you will be empowered, equipped, and laser-focused to succeed. So come along on this adventure with me and learn how my experiences in life made me a Perception Buster!

"Everyone can rise above their circumstances and achieve success if they are dedicated to and passionate about what they do." – Nelson Mandela

INTRODUCTION

This book presents a new way to overcome the challenges in your life. From what I've discovered, when your purpose and passion are in alignment with your livelihood, it becomes your calling, and you can see your life becoming a dream. Being the second son in my family, I understood that you could have 20/20 vision and still be blind.

The pain I carried while growing up was not my own. I was 5 years old when my brother Carl passed away. After his death, there were times when my father would take me out for fishing, and give me a beer. Dr. Deantoni shared with me that at a very young age, I became my Dad's drinking buddy and my mother's therapist. I discovered that pain was like a ball of yarn that must be untangled. Grief can make you emotionally unavailable. In the sixties, there was not any grief counseling or support that people could use to deal with their mental suffering. So for my family, the grieving process was left unaddressed, which exacerbated my mental suffering as the second oldest son.

As I busted my negative perceptions growing up, I discovered that mistakes are experiences that help you to grow. And as Dennis Waitley said, "Failure should be our teacher, not our undertaker. Failure should be considered as a delay, not defeat. It is a temporary detour, not a dead end."

I don't consider failure as a waste of my time and efforts if I end up learning something valuable from the entire experience. One of my favorite quotes from Nelson Mandela is: "Do not judge me by my successes, judge me by how many times I fell down and got back up again."

As a man who went through great loss and grief, my passion as a Perception Buster is for you, my readers, to fully understand that we all will have pains, and if we don't learn how to transform them, we will always be passing them on to others.

CHAPTER 01 | TAKE DECISIVE ACTION

"Change your thoughts, and you change your world." –
Norman Vincent Peale

Henry David Thoreau quotes that when a man or woman advances in the direction of their dreams and attempt to live that dream in their imagination, they will meet with a success unexpected in common hours. They'll work on new thoughts and put old thoughts behind them. They will advance toward an invisible boundary because of their commitment.

Providence does its magic when you commit to yourself. It removes all sorts of things that might hinder your way. There was a point in my life when I had to take decisive action regarding a justice-involved predicament as a veteran and was encouraged to go into a treatment program.

I was going to prison for the 2nd time over a 30-year period, because of my disease of alcoholism. During the deliberations, prior to being announced, I understood that I was on my way to prison. I also knew that politics had a big role to play in this. However, I also acknowledged that God must've had a plan for me, and there might be some good awaiting me even in a place like a prison. That's the thing about faith. Your heart remains at peace even though you know you have a seemingly insurmountable obstacle right in front of you. Hence, my faith was at a point where the thought of going to prison didn't panic me. I believed in God, and knew that He was sufficient for me.

I was sentenced to 8 years and 8 months in prison this time around. And during this period, I didn't have any accidents, zero injuries, and no harm on my record, whatsoever. As an honorably discharged 100% service-connected (top-tier) Navy veteran suffering from PTSD and 30% migraines, the judge sent me to prison anyway. Even when I had an official letter from the Department of Veteran Affairs that prison would not be a remedy for my disease of alcoholism.

VA Medical Center
 10535 Hospital Way, Mather, CA 95655
Community Living Center (CLC)
 150 Muir Road, Martinez, CA 94553
VA Outpatient Clinics:
 2221 Martin Luther King, Jr. Way, Oakland, CA 94612
 150 Muir Road, Martinez, CA 94553
 103 Bodin Circle, Bldg. 778, Travis AFB, CA 94535
 Building 201, Walnut Avenue, Mare Island, CA 94592

VA Outpatient Clinics (cont.)
 280 Cohasset Road, Chico, CA 95926
 5342 Dudley Avenue, McClellan, CA 95652
 351 Hartnell Avenue, Redding, CA 96002
Oakland Behavioral Health Clinic
 525 21st Street, Oakland, CA 94612
Telephone Care: 1-800-382-8387
Website: www.northern-california.med.va.gov

Department of Veterans Affairs
VA Northern California Health Care System (VANCHCS)
10535 Hospital Way, Mather, CA 95655

March 27, 2013

Dear Your Honor:

I am the Veterans Justice Outreach Specialist (VJOS) for the VA Northern California Health Care System. One of my roles is to facilitate timely access to VA services and benefits to justice-involved Veterans and to act as a liaison between the VA and the court. I am writing this letter on behalf of Veteran, Ryland Hill. This writer interviewed Mr. Hill in custody and he has expressed an interest in residential treatment at Sacramento Veterans Resource Center (SVRC), funded by the Department of Veterans Affairs. He can receive residential substance recovery services for up to six months, provided he remains focused on treatment and continues to adhere to the program rules. Once he completes his stay on the treatment side of the program, he can move to the Transitional Living Program (TLP), on the same campus, where he can receive services for an additional two years. Services at the Transitional Living Program are geared toward maintaining the Veterans recovery gains, obtaining gainful employment and locating permanent, stable housing. This writer has opined that Mr. Hill is an appropriate candidate for this program and he has been placed on a waiting list.

Once there is an available treatment bed at SVRC, this VJOS can facilitate placement, monitor treatment compliance, and report progress to the court as requested. SVRC works closely with the Veteran in terms of allowing the Veteran to attend Court dates and can directly communicate with the court as needed, once a release of information has been signed by the Veteran.

Mr. Hill would greatly appreciate the opportunity to address the issues that contributed to his criminal justice involvement and has verbalized responsibility for the choices he made that has lead to his current situation. If you should have any questions or concerns pertaining to Mr. Hill's proposed treatment options, please contact me at (916) 843.9237.

Best Regards,

Sue Cooper, LCSW
Veterans Justice Outreach Specialist
916.843.9237
Suzanne.cooper3@va.gov

While in county jail, and throughout my time going in and out of the system, I led hundreds of men on the right path, helping them to connect and get closer to the Lord, held praise, and worship services, and conducted many Bible studies in different jails and was also chosen by Chaplains to assist other inmates as well.

All the while, I knew that God was using this reputation of mine to keep me safe in prison. Eventually, I was also asked to do a Thursday Bible Study in Soledad by the shot-callers. God informed me that Soledad actually stood for something: Seeing Our Lord Every Day Annihilating Depression. The judge was, of course, not aware that God wanted me to take advantage of this stay by attending Seminary.

I soon became a Tumi student. The Board of Prison Hearing overruled the DA's conviction because of the strong support from my brother, sister, the community, and the entire Tumi staff. I left the prison as a Tumi student, a non-violent inmate who earned many positive achievements. I had a 3.8 average in Seminary, and as you can see, I exceeded expectations. Consequently, I was released 6 years early! Isn't that amazing?

Reflection allows you to learn from your failures and mistakes. I committed myself to this legal situation I found myself in and invoked my right to defend myself. In Soledad, I found a book named 'Win Your Case,' written by Gerry Spence. He states, "As a citizen who has suffered injustice, it's better to 'lose fighting' than to give up because one cannot get proper representation to lie down in the Battle of Life. It's not only to lose the battle but to 'lose the self.'"

It's amazing how you get crystal clear vision when you choose to trust in the self. During the process, I remembered why I chose to defend myself. All the experiences I was involved in came back to help me. It was unbelievable. The current situation I found myself in made me recall many similar experiences that I had previously. One such situation resembles greatly like that of Joseph in the Bible. When I was in the fifth grade, my principal, Mr. Ray Armstrong, chose me from the entire Ralph J Bunche School to go to see Santa Claus as I was the nicest and the smartest kid there. I was given 500 dollars' worth of presents for the holiday. Jacob gave Joseph a coat of different colors. His brothers sold him into slavery, then Potiphar's wife attempted to seduce Joseph, and he ended up in prison. This story was one that encouraged me a lot. Furthermore, I learned of this story at a very crucial time in my life, when I was myself litigating my case. So it will always hold a special place in my heart. I could see myself relating to some of the aspects of Joseph's life, and it helped me to stay strong and more resilient.

Another special circumstance took place when I was in the Navy. I was the captain of the football team, just like I was in High School. We were 29-0 and were playing the Championship Marines in Hawaii and as a

Captain, I was the night baker onboard the ship. At that time, I wasn't required to play because everybody knew I worked a 12-hours shift and slept during the day. On the day of the big game, my teammates came to my bunk and begged me to play as they needed someone on their team urgently. I, obviously, refused to be a part of the game since I was already so exhausted from all the baking at night. They insisted and said that if I didn't bring the excitement and the lively energy they knew that I had as their captain, they would not be able to win the game. I was humbled but also blown away when they said this to me. It never dawned on me that my contribution would play such a significant role! I remember that this experience played a pivotal role for me as I learned how to stay positive in a place where they relegate you as worthless and powerless. In life, there are many occasions when you feel people looking down upon you, considering you someone who doesn't "belong" or doesn't conform to the "societal standards" set by society. In times like these and otherwise, I began to be more confident and comfortable as I started to believe in the powers and capabilities I hold within, without paying much heed to what others have to say about me.

RYLAND GEORGE HILL JR.
"Sugar-Mouth"
General Course
Freshman Football; Freshman
Basketball; Reserve Football, Reserve
Basketball; Varsity Football (1 yr.)
Career

In conclusion, I soon started a basketball group/ministry in Chico, California, where 98.7 percent of that community was white at Seventh Day Adventist Church with a Superior Court Judge, a general surgeon, a podiatrist, and physical therapist who were all white men and very humble but also very competitive. At the same time, I served as a President of a non-profit called New Unity. For 4 years, the experience with this community made me very comfortable in the courtroom, where I saw the most so-called fierce, powerful men turn into scared children in front of the judge whereas I was quite confident. A sweet Italian lady who is no longer with us named Clarise Salsa picked me up to replace her for the convalescent ministry in Chico. I first refused but then, I recalled my Missionary grandmother made me attend her meetings growing up, and I hated those boring meetings. Clarise told me after observing me for 4 years that I was all-heart. I believe my grandmother played a trick on me because when I shared how much I hated my grandmother's missionary meetings. The elderly would all laugh out loud. After three years, my children would also come with me to attend those meetings.

Collectively, the different aspects of my life revolving around the ministries, having won a forensic speech contest at Chico State, working as an Account Executive for Yellow Pages, my worship services and Bible studies in prison time, etc., all contributed to my early release.

Now, let me share with you that when you are in jail, there is a saying that an inmate who represents himself has a "fool" for an attorney. I heard that small voice in my head telling me that "I never lost a case, Pastor Ryland." I said, "Excuse me, Lord. You know I have been arrested in front of my apartment door twice in the last two months." He said, "You're going to represent yourself." So when the trailing Judge Brown called and said, "Mr. Hill, are you ready to move forward?" I replied, "Your Honor, I am no longer Mr. Hill. I am Pastor Hill, and my addiction to alcoholism is in remission."

The courtroom was packed with attorneys and had gone eerily silent. If I was God, I would have never chosen myself as a Pastor. I then realized I was carrying around an immense amount of others' pain. While being away, I received therapy from a gifted psychologist, Dr. Deantoni. Yes, I did lose at trial, but what gave me peace was that my case was reversed and modified on Governor's Brown choice of a committed returning citizen who worked hard. I was released six years early. And I remembered the words of God when he said that he never lost a case. And my belief in him strengthened more than ever.

My victory was only possible when I changed the way I saw my dire situation. No matter the odds, I continued to overcome all the challenges that came my way. I busted my perception by taking decisive action at the right time, and success, therefore, became inevitable.

There are times when people encounter a very difficult situation in life that makes them feel stuck. It seems to them as if there is no way up and no way down as if they're trapped, and the doors they're pounding on seem too rigid to budge. And that's when the panicking starts too. Most people find it hard to keep their cool in such situations. Hardships, obstacles, trials, and tribulations always come unannounced, and it is this very nature of it that adds to the gravity of one's problems.

There never has been a situation that stayed tough forever. Things get simpler with time; they get better. Nothing is permanent, and nothing is meant to last till the end. In times like these and otherwise, one must remember to believe in themselves because it really does wonders. Self-belief helps in kicking into gear the psychological processes that push us to achieve our goals. If you lack self-confidence, then even if your situation is manageable, you will find it extremely burdensome, almost insurmountable.

Your state of mind has a very important role to play in this aspect. I've learned to optimize the power of self-belief to take control of my life and become the best version of myself, the authentic version!

CHAPTER 02 | IN THE FURNACE

When I was at Soledad University, I was struck by a massive change in my perception. Steve, a believer who I came across at Soledad University, quoted the following while we were walking around the track in Soledad. "I found out that jails and prisons were not made for humans. The walls of the prison did not confine a person; rather, they were created to confine a 'mentality.'" Limiting a toxic belief, a mindset, and eradicating evil thoughts was what jails were designed to do.

This realization led me to another important realization. I pondered over the power of mindsets and belief systems and how they can define the experiences we have, shaping them in molds of positive perspectives or negative perspectives. The challenges I faced in my life allowed me to develop a very different take on the trials and tribulations that we go through. I came to the conclusion that we do our best when we're going through trials in our lives! Difficulties give you a precise, clear view of who you are. They bring out the warrior in you, the fighter in you. We may not be aware of the strength we hold within us unless we are exposed to hurdles and tribulations. Once we are forged into the furnace, we uncover our full potential and, in doing so, might even surprise our ownselves as we begin to realize what all we can endure and how resilient we really are.

Me going into the furnace heightened my perception. It's essential to have an accurate view of yourself because, as Dr. Martin Luther King said, "The ultimate measure of a man is not where he stands in moments of comfort and convenience, but where he stands at times of challenge and controversy."

If we take the example of Daniel in the Bible, we learn that he was in a state of peace and calmness in the lion's den, even everybody else around him was worrying. This is a story from which we all can learn from. It tells us that if you have a lion's den in your life currently, then God will help you out of it and be with you through it all, till the very end! While being in the lion's den, you must declare that you will not live up to the "low expectations," considering yourself inferior by thinking you're an inmate, prisoner, or convict. By busting your perceptions, you are using your voice and declaring you will not be limited by the house you were raised in. Sometimes our past, our upbringing, and the circumstances that we have faced in life become our biggest hindrance, and only by busting our perception can we begin to defy all odds and be the person we have always wanted to be. Let nothing obstruct your path to your destination. It requires you to go out of your way and walk an extra mile; go for it. Put in every bit of your effort so, at the end of the day, you don't hold any kind of regret thinking you didn't give your best shot.

Righteousness or any act of doing good is the "cure for the insecure." While being in the furnace, you are likely to encounter such situations that you might never have experienced before. These situations will test you greatly and might even make you vulnerable and weak if you don't learn how to bust your perception to help you in those troubling times. During such moments, you must remember that you are *not* alone. You have a God who is watching over you at all times. He's aware of even the smallest bits of difficulties happening in your life, so don't think for a second that you're all by yourself. You can count on God, have faith in Him, and you'll never be disappointed.

In the same way, God has appointed people from among us who we can also rely on. There are plenty of people waiting to have someone help them make their lives count for something," to make it meaningful. I declared I would keep growing while in the furnace. While drinking, driving, and doing my daily activities, I could now see that I allowed my emotions to be exalted "above my decisions." You can be in your own way self-made-prison, or you can be in a real one!

Seeing things God's way is hard and painful because we don't have the ability to truly understand the power of His supreme plans for us. Just like Jonah, I found that God threw me overboard as a tired, reluctant servant to embrace his love. Jonah knew this very well after being swallowed by the big fish, that he could not do anything within his capacity to escape from the big fish. He just trusted the process and relied on no one but God. In my case, the big fish was the entire court system I was trapped in. I, too, relied on God and had faith in His mercy.

Ask yourself, what does it look like when you're faced with a controversy? You intuitively yearn for somebody's help. So I decided to get professional help and received therapy for 3 years. I also attended AA Al-anon, Domestic Violence Training, attended Seminary, and stayed in top shape. My time in the furnace was spent interacting with those people only who wanted to be proactive in moving forward in their lives. I remained faithful and positive in the Chapel. In other words, I "perceived" I was becoming who I already was! Isn't that amazing? I realized that pressure pushed me to embrace a totally different perspective, one that I had never uncovered previously! I was turning my test into my testimony for the outside. I was not just living, but I was living with passion! And when you are living with passion, then gratitude automatically becomes your second nature. Paying gratitude is a very positive action to adopt in life because it opens doors of peace and bliss. The more you pay gratitude to God, the more you start to acknowledge all the things that God blessed you with. You start to notice how even the smallest thing in your life has a purpose and how much you depend on it.

My awareness of the immense amount of pain that I was carrying could have compelled me to pass it on to another. I could have transmitted that pain to someone else, to my family, or to any acquaintance and be accused of vehicular manslaughter or, in my case, murder. I was totally convinced that the wrong choices I made, made me an enemy of myself. It was my choice not to take the judge's advice. It was my choices that led me to a black-out period. As humans, we are bound to err. We make mistakes and make them over and over again. None of us are perfect, and none can claim to be because we are all flawed in some way. What matters is your determination to change your flawed self. What matters is the will to become a better version of yourself. We all need deliverance from our past choices, our personal hang-ups, and bad habits! After all, this is how a person evolves over time.

No more fast and easy for Ryland; I started my healing process. I healed and untangled the wounds that were deep inside me by going consistently to Dr. Deantoni for therapy. Deep-satisfying became the norm. By overcoming my past mistakes to address future decisions, I forged myself into a man of integrity. My behavior kept me from feeling inferior as I chose to now forgive myself and maintain my dignity as a veteran with Honorable Discharge in spite of being in an environment where the whole system was designed to make you feel inferior. This is a process that gives you credibility, authority, and moral superiority. It's oppressive and soul-destroying to be motivated by hate, so I was convicted of starting a Thursday afternoon Bible study right on X-wing for three years. You see, having litigated my own case prior to coming to prison made me aware that I was walking by faith! Trusting God is so fulfilling. I was released six years early before my release date, which was this year, 2022. Miracles happen when you decide to leave your matters to God. The things we assume impossible are actually very easy for God, so why not leave out all our worries and entrust God, who holds control and power over literally everything?

With God's assistance by your side, you can see yourself changing your negative emotions by doing things you love, for example, reading, writing, going to the gym, starting a new project, and bringing out the creativity in yourself. How you see things determine the outcome of your destiny! I had busted my negative perception, and ever since then, my life has not remained the same way. It has changed magnificently, and I'm grateful and happy for it.

CHAPTER 03 | BE THE WORK

The brain is quite a strange organ of the human body. It's fed with tons of information; it notes all the advice you get, even taking note of everything that is good for you and of all things that don't benefit us in any way. But despite all that the brain already knows, it only takes a moment for an idea to click. And when that click is made, the information that you already knew, and knew for quite some time, starts to actually settle in your mind. It's almost as if the brain has just begun to comprehend the importance of the knowledge it used to harbor. It's only when the click is made does the brain start to process that information, compelling us to finally take action and implement.

Such a click happened to me when I was in prison. My mindset started to change as I realized that alcoholism is a numbing agent. Of course, I've always known how damaging alcohol is to our body, mind, and soul, but it was while lying alone in my cell that it truly hit me that alcohol is of no good to me. In fact, it has done nothing but destroy the peace of my mind, damage my personality and render me a man who can't even trust his own memory. Where did I go so wrong that I started to seek solace and comfort in something that is so dangerous, offering not a single benefit and still keeping me hooked to it?

The realization that hit me that day struck me when I looked at the problem from a different perspective. I thought about my future generations. This wasn't just about me; it was about the generations that would come after me! What will they think about their forefather? What message am I giving to the next generation? What would they think of me? A wasted old man who kept ending up in prison just because he couldn't quit drinking?

This newfound perception of mine made me overcome my addiction. Alcoholism was something that I was struggling with for years, something that I always thought was impossible for me to quit, but I was able to really get over this self-damaging addiction once I viewed it as problematic from the perspective of other people, that is, the generation to come.

This shift in my mindset was followed by another stark realization that dawned on me. I figured out the one thing that really impacts one's ability to change. I discovered yet another significant factor that compels a person to go the extra mile and do a bit more than usual. I recognized the power that peer pressure plays in one's life and how it can actually serve as the biggest motivation ever.

Peer pressure is an area of concern when you attempt to bust your perception and be the work! Most of what we do, our demeanor, habits, actions, and efforts, are inspired by societal practices and standards. We want to be accepted by our peers. We yearn for approval from the people around us, hoping to comply with our actions in accordance with the standards set by society. We're focused on pleasing people, and for some of us, the biggest nightmare is getting rejected by people. To me, this thought process helped me in getting rid of a toxic habit. But there are times when the fear of peer pressure can actually take a toll on your belief system, instilling a fear deep down inside that makes you restless.

What we fail to ponder over is the fact that people do not bless us; God does. So whose opinion should matter to us? God or some random stranger who doesn't even know anything about us, our struggles, the challenges we go through, or the dilemmas we face in our everyday lives? Should we be focused on pleasing people, or should we focus on pleasing God? Ask yourself this, which is more important?

You please God when you follow His commandments and do those things that He instructed us to do. As a result, our life starts to take a turn for the better, and we see that God is blessing us. On the contrary, pleasing people is an impossible task. One day you make them happy, and the other, you find them objecting and frustrated over the smallest thing. Thriving to make people happy is like getting stuck in a loop that doesn't seem to stop. So why chase it? Why build our happiness on getting approvals from people who don't even matter to us?

Such kind of a mindset is based on negative perceptions. When you find yourself constantly surrounded by negative thoughts that are impacting your mental state, know that you need to take a break. Don't rush yourself. You don't have to involve yourself in this mindless rat race. Rather, work on your own self. Take your time and walk your path. You're not running out of time. Don't let people trick you into believing that there is a certain age by which you should accomplish a certain task. Move at your own pace. There's only you on the path to your destination, so comparing it with others becomes pointless.

A heads-up; when you begin to challenge your negative perceptions, you will again be misunderstood by people. And I say this from experience because when I went all out and started to bust my negative perceptions, I saw people around me raising eyebrows and questioning my belief system. This is dangerous because it makes us doubt ourselves. And when self-doubts start to take root in you, know that you need to get rid of those as early as possible. Start to de-throne your own opinion, and then declare, 'I will be the highest and the best version of myself!' No more budgeting your own thinking!

I have always been the kind of person who believed in paving a path traveled by none. I chose to be a trendsetter, and I grew up admiring people who had this ability to set trends, stand out among the rest, and do the extraordinary. I like breaking all of my old negative beliefs and rules that restrict me from doing things I want to do.

God has used the worst moments to bring out the best methods, that is, Busting Perceptions! It is when you are at your lowest do you truly begin to see what this life is all about. The reality starts to sink in at that time because, at that moment, there are no distractions. It's just you and the reality of life staring at you right in your face. You better take your thoughts seriously when you reach this stage because when you're vulnerable and weak, it is only God who is trying to lift you back up. You'll only find God at your side and no one else. This stage could be the turning point of your life; when you have the chance to redeem yourself and turn over a new leaf.

In that moment, you should be willing to do the ridiculous! Consider every day as a new opportunity to 'Be the Work' in your own life. If you have to thrive, go forward with the plan and make things happen. It doesn't matter where your location is; as long as you're constantly moving and checking off things from your task list, you are moving in the right direction.

On your way, you might come across many unpleasant experiences. There will be obstacles and hindrances as big as mountains, for the path to greatness is never too easy to travel. The roadmap won't be smooth, nobody guarantees it to be so, but you just don't have to suck on the bitter lemons in your life. Try to concentrate on the sweet blessings God has bestowed upon you. This will make you grateful for all things that you possess, and you will not lose yourself amidst the hardships that is only there temporarily, and you will certainly be able to finish well!

To reach the finish line, you must remove self-centered 'strongholds' that are there in your mind. God loves it when we take our mess and turn it into a loving message. He, in fact, encourages us to find our weaknesses and acknowledge that we have a weakness because only then can we start to eliminate those weaknesses.

I came to understand that criminalizing alcoholism is all wrong. It's a spiritual and medical condition that can be treated. Your greatest obstacle is your greatest opportunity. When you are strong enough to withstand the elements, you are going to be exposed too! You will be revealed. You will be brought out of hiding by God.

Furthermore, I found that defying my inner critic is a life-long challenge. Due to my reluctance to accept my calling, God chose to give me the opportunity to decide my destiny to "Bust my own Perception" about myself!

CHAPTER 04 | FEAR IS REAL

The reason why I decided to write a book was my understanding that there are many aspects of my life from which other people could benefit from. I've lived a life that most may not familiarize themselves with; nevertheless, the experiences I've gone through are definitely stories that people can relate some aspects of their lives with, taking some valuable takeaways from it too.

The part of my life I'm going to discuss in this chapter will shed light on my after-retirement phase from the Navy. This part of my life is, in many ways, important to me. During this period, there were some decisions that I never regretted making; in fact, I actually feel proud that I did make them, despite the odds.

After the Navy, I decided to go back to college when I was 29. I was thinking about it for some time when I finally decided that learning new things would help me become more conscientious and more present-minded. I was always of the opinion that knowledge and learning shouldn't be restricted to a certain age. We're all in the process of growing and learning. We all *should* broaden our minds and the scope of our thought-process and educate ourselves to come to new understandings and explore the unexplored.

What did I learn from the time I spent at college is something that cannot be summarized that easily, for there are numerous things that I learned, most of which were concepts which I had never before comprehended with such great depth. One of the many things I truly developed an understanding of was the notion of fear.

In college, I got the opportunity to address my class on this very topic. Although I, in many respects, was dissimilar to my classmates, I focused my speech on something that I believed I shared with all the undergraduates – fear. Back then, in the '90s, incoming freshmen often reported their anxiety prior to entering college. The transition from high school to college brought different fears to the surface. Likewise, students who returned to college after many years of absence reported similar fears.

College freshmen found it difficult to identify exactly where the problem lay. As a re-entry student myself, I also, to some extent, experienced the same difficulty and wanted to persuade other people that it's essential to be aware of the subtle effect that fear has on each and every one of us in each class we take.

Eleanor Roosevelt once quoted an unknown author by saying, "You gain strength, courage, and confidence by every experience in which you… stop to look fear in the face… You must do the thing you think you cannot do."

For my speech, I chose to discuss precisely this because I knew that this is a feeling that everyone held within, whether they acknowledged it or not. To address the problem, I looked at some reasons why the fear of failure, the fear of the unknown, and self-fulfilling prophecies had paralyzed freshmen students from achieving their full potential. I also analyzed the causes that trigger the harmful effects that fear could produce.

I learned that freshmen students developed fears that created doubt. A common fear was the fear of failure. Some students doubted their ability to succeed at the college level. These students had often received negative feedback throughout their elementary and high-school years. They suffered from low self-esteem and were insecure about their new academic experience.

As per my observation, students in their first year have the potential to do well in school, but usually, they underachieve, and they may be afraid to make mistakes. But in the counseling center at Berkeley's Writer's College, students were told that making mistakes was important. It's considered a way of learning about one's strengths and what worked well for them and what did not work well. It's only when we do not learn from our mistakes and refuse to correct them that they become failures. As Robert Steinberg wrote in 1986, "People don't thrive to attain their full potential because they fail to face the important challenges in life."

Students of all generations tend to spend a lot of energy and time dodging the system and their work as assigned due to the fear of failure.

After the examination of the crippling effect that fear of failure produces, let's dig deeper and understand another reason why fear plays such a pivotal role in the lack of freshmen success. And this also goes for students belonging to different eras and coming from different backgrounds.

Instead of high school counselors making students see that they have the potential to achieve, they make predictions about certain students as if they're a prophet predicting their very future. Well-meaning counselors sometimes steer students away from attending college. They advise the students to consider the workforce instead. In today's economy, jobs today call for more than just a high school diploma. The students receive a "can't do" message, further lowering their self-esteem. Often, this leads to a cycle of low grades, fulfilling the prophecies of failure.

Robert Steinberg's book *Intelligence Applied* explains why intelligent people may fail. Steinberg had identified stumbling blocks that get in the way of even the brightest and the sharpest of freshman students and prevent them from becoming academically successful. "It scarcely matters what talents people have if they are not motivated to use them," he writes.

First-semester students relied on the correctness of their college professors. Students were still immature and relied on others for their external rewards. But a lot of students said that immaturity had nothing to do with their grades here at Chico State University. Steinberg states, "A lack of self-confidence gnaws away at a person's ability to get things done, and this becomes a self-fulfilling prophecy." It's all in your mind.

Now that we understand how self-fulfilling prophecies can create fear in freshmen students, let's take a brief look at the fear of the unknown and see how it can be a deterrent to our success, especially the success of first-year students and attempting a new experience.

Any new experience that one knows little about can be really scary. On holidays and birthdays, for instance, we receive unknown gifts that are new and different, yet we don't fear those types of gifts, do we? Yet maybe it all lies in the way one packages things. An attractive package that we are expecting is the one that we look forward to receiving. I firmly believe that there is beauty and joy in the gift called New Experience!

CHAPTER 05 | SAY 'YES' TO NEW OPPORTUNITIES

One of the greatest threats that fear poses to a person is its overpowering ability to take over a person's mind. Once it does, you lose control over that fear as it continues to grow stronger, grasping your thoughts and disrupting creative intellect. Hence, having enough power to limit your fears is essential if you have great things planned in life. You cannot let your fears hinder your path to greatness.

Here, I'd like to stress on the fact that fears *can* be eliminated if you know how to deal with them. As a person who battled many fears during the course of my lifetime, I can assert that you can *trick* your fears. If you know how to tackle them, you can then get in a position where fears no longer have the power to take over your good conscience. And you can only be able to accomplish this if you have a strong mind frame that *believes* you can!

We can see how fear of the unknown can disguise itself as a problem. Let's discuss three solutions that can be very helpful in combatting fears that we usually face in our lives, especially as students who aspire to perform well in their studies.

1. Accepting New Challenges:

The first is to identify some traits that define a successful student. Successful students tend to be risk takers. The process of getting enrolled in college is a risk to some, yet they do it regardless, and that's how they take the first step towards success. By saying successful students, I don't mean students who never failed in life. Successful students are those who might have failed once or twice, or maybe even more than this but never backed down. These are students who were determined to keep on trying again and again until they succeeded. These are students who have a knack for learning from their mistakes. Remember, you're not a failure if you're willing to correct your mistakes and learn from them. Viewing each failure as a stepping stone to success is a remarkable perception to develop. It indicates how a person's mind is inclined to positive things in life, thereby attracting positivity, bliss, and happiness. People who recognize their successes and overcome their failures eventually reach their goals, no matter what.

Those who want to accomplish their goals at all costs do not hesitate to take risks. They do not fear new experiences. On the contrary, they try not to let any new opportunity slide by because they are well aware of how important it is to learn new things in order to grow and evolve. After all, the goal is not to ace every opportunity but to avail every opportunity you get and make the most of it. This is the real success, and this is how a champion's mindset should be programmed to think and perceive.

2. Embrace the Challenges Beforehand

The second solution is that we must take things as a challenge. For example, if you start to view your college life as a roller coaster ride that has its ups and downs, you will be spared the 'surprise' element whenever you do encounter a downfall. As long as we believe that life is going to return to the top again, we can rise to the challenge, and we can persevere. The hope that you will rise again after hitting a new low is what will keep you going. This 'hope' is pivotal for you as it would help you thrive and move forward amidst all the hurdles.

By considering every unique situation as a challenge, you are bound to foresee the worst of the worst scenarios that you may encounter. You are not taken aback by the gravity of a particular situation because you have already planned it as a potential challenge. You are not caught off guard; rather, you had seen it all coming. Therefore, no matter how difficult a circumstance appears, you'd be able to deal with it efficiently because a part of your mind must have prepared itself to embrace such adversities beforehand.

3. Healthy Outlook Guarantees Successful Outcome

Lastly, we can envision our future. We must see ourselves as successful people. We must believe that we will, one day, be successful. This belief will help you survive even in the most crucial of times. So even if things become blurry, and even when you're losing your focus, you can maintain the ability to fine-tune your life and become even more goal-directed.

The important point here is that wherever you are, whatever you will become, directly depends on your state of mind and the kind of thought process harboring in your brain. Half of the work is done by the mind. Your belief system needs to be strong enough that it compels you to walk an extra mile each time you set out to achieve your goals.

As it is said, "But sooner or later, the man who wins is the man who thinks he can."

We must have faith in ourselves and stay persistent and willing to keep thriving despite all odds. When we don't succeed the first time, we can analyze our faults and search for solutions until we are successful. It is difficult for many students to appreciate their own success. Successful students have learned to celebrate their victories, but most importantly, they have learned to overcome their college fears.

To summarize, we have discussed the reasons why fear is real among college freshmen, and we came up with practical solutions to overcome it. Successful freshmen students are confident enough to believe in themselves, but most importantly, they expect their classmates to appreciate their abilities.

As Eleanor Roosevelt reminds us, while thinking about overcoming our college fears, "You gain strength, courage, and confidence by every experience in which you… stop to look fear in the face… You must do the thing you think you cannot do. You must do the thing you think you cannot do."

CONCLUSION

If there's one thing that is deeply-rooted and common in the lives of people, it's the uncertainty factor of life. We can never be too sure about what the future has in store for us. We can never know what we might have to face in the next stage of our life, no matter how hard we try. There's nothing much we can do to figure out a risk-free life, avoid obstacles, and live a life without any challenges, because the element of uncertainty is always there to surprise us.

My life has taught me numerous lessons. But the learning that I consider to be most important is having an unwavering, resolute, and unshakeable belief in God and His plans. We might not have an inkling of where we are headed or what we are going to encounter ahead, but knowing that God is watching over you and observing every little injustice happening to you, you should know that you're not alone.

With a firm belief in God's plans for us, we no longer need to worry, for we will surely make our way out of every adverse situation through His guidance and help. Just imagine you have the assistance of a being in whose hands is the entire dominion and who is competent over all things. Whatever it is that we're worrying about is something very simple in His eyes, for nothing is impossible for Him to do.

Trust God, follow your instincts, and understand that no obstacle will last forever. Every hurdle in life is temporary, and you will, at the end of the day, reach the light at the end of the tunnel.

Made in the USA
Middletown, DE
11 April 2023

28508997R00024